·FUN·WITH·MATHS·

PROBLEM SOLVING

LAKSHMI HEWAVISENTI

Gloucester Press
London · New York · Toronto · Sydney

Created and designed by
N.W. Books
28 Percy Street
London W1P 9FF

Design: David West
Children's Book Design
Editor: Melanie Halton
Illustrators: John Kelly
Ian Moores

First published in Great Britain in 1991 by
Franklin Watts Ltd
96 Leonard Street
London
EC2A 4RH

ISBN 0-7496-0559-6

Printed in Belgium

A CIP catalogue record for this book is available from the British Library.

CONTENTS

INTRODUCTION

There are lots of problems and activities in this book which you will enjoy solving and sharing. They are fun to do, and with each activity you'll have learnt something new about maths. They also give you ideas which you could use to make up your own problems – for others to solve!

FRUIT CARDS

Here is a game you can play with a friend, where fruits represent numbers. This means that you can use them to solve problems. Each fruit card will be worth a certain number.

What you need

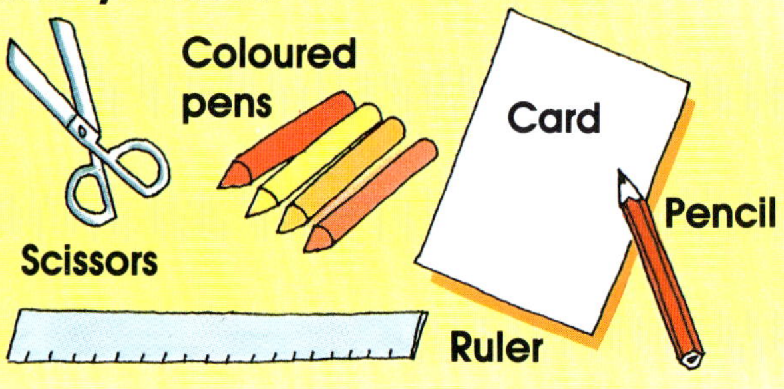

How to make it
Draw a grid like the one shown here. Use a ruler to make sure all the sections are the same size.

Draw your cards
Use your pens to colour in the fruit. Now cut out the cards.

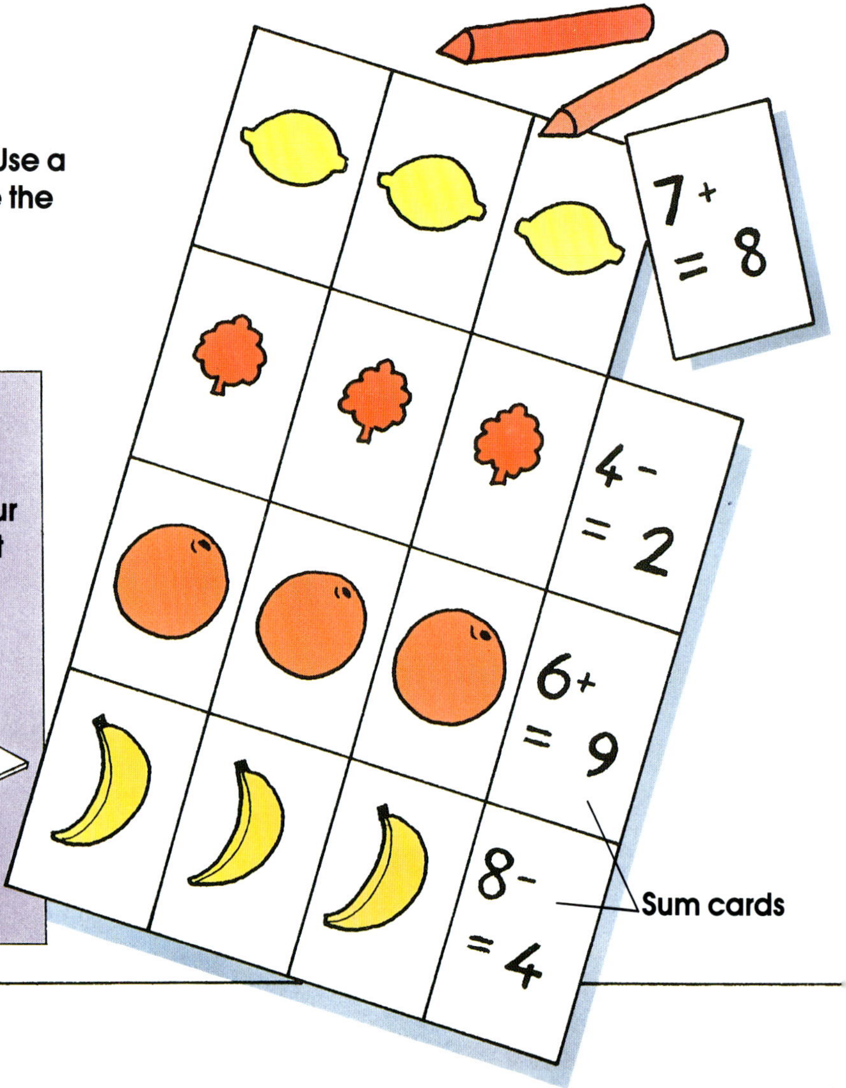

How to play
Take out the "sum cards" and share out the rest. Now turn over a sum card and take turns to show the fruit which will make the sum work.

Fruit numbers
Look at the table below to find out how much each fruit card is worth:

You could make up more problems, and think up some new fruit cards. This would make the game longer, more interesting and... harder!

COUNTING CAKES

Cooking can be a lot of fun. Before you start you must work out how much of everything you will need. We have given the amounts for four people. Can you work out how much you will need for eight people?

You need eggs, flour, sugar, butter and cherries. These are the "ingredients".

Baking for four
This chart shows how much of each ingredient you need to make four cakes.

Eggs		2
Flour		6
Sugar		3
Butter		1
Cherries		4

FOUR MORE FRIENDS ARRIVE

Baking for eight
Copy the chart and fill in how much you need.

Eggs	
Flour	
Sugar	
Butter	
Cherries	

Now if four more people decide to come, how much of each ingredient will you need?

Can you work out the ingredients needed for 12, 16 or 20 people? How do you work these out?

HOW MUCH OF EACH INGREDIENT WILL YOU NEED FOR 12 PEOPLE?

CAKE FRACTIONS

Can you imagine having a party where one cake has to be eaten by 100 people? Well, everyone will get a tiny piece! But if only four people share it, they should get decent portions!

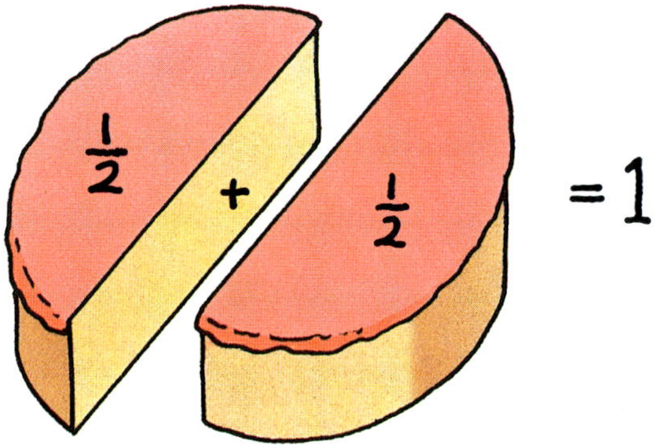

If a cake is cut into two pieces, each piece is called a half (½). Two halves make a whole cake.

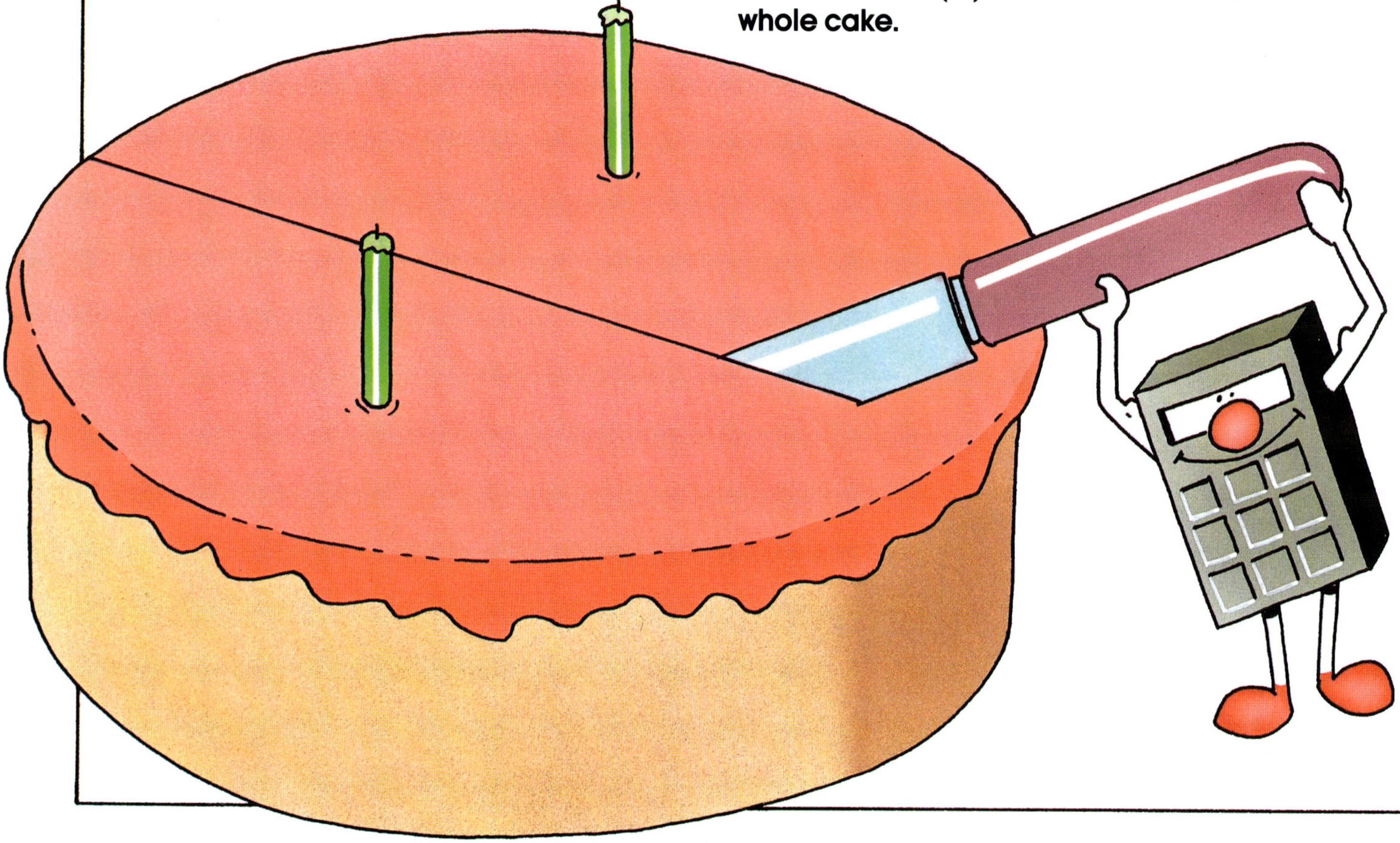

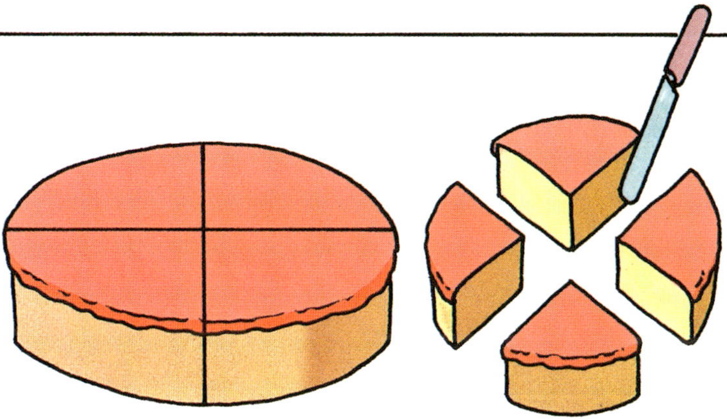

$$\frac{1}{4} = \frac{\text{ONE PIECE}}{\text{FOUR PIECES}}$$

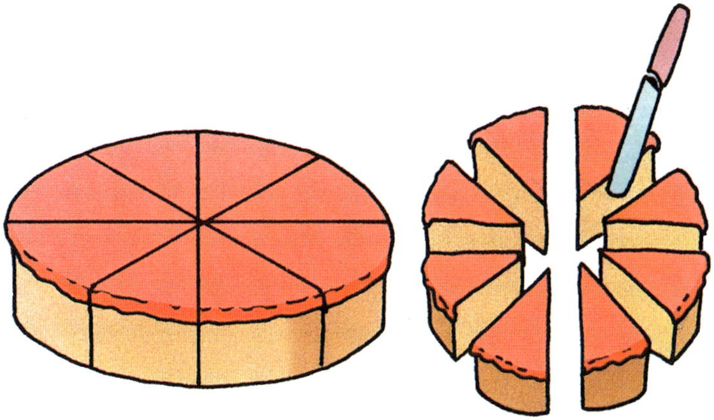

$$\frac{1}{8} = \frac{\text{ONE PIECE}}{\text{EIGHT PIECES}}$$

If you cut a cake into eight pieces, how many of these would you need to make half a cake? How many pieces would give you a quarter of the cake? How many would give you two whole cakes?

If you can't work it out, turn to page 32.

WATER MUSIC

Have you ever tried making music with glasses of water? In this activity we're going to measure out different amounts and try to make up a tune. Use identical glasses.

How to make it

Start by filling up one of your four glasses with water. Make sure it reaches the top.

Now pour half of this into another glass. Leave one of these glasses on the side.

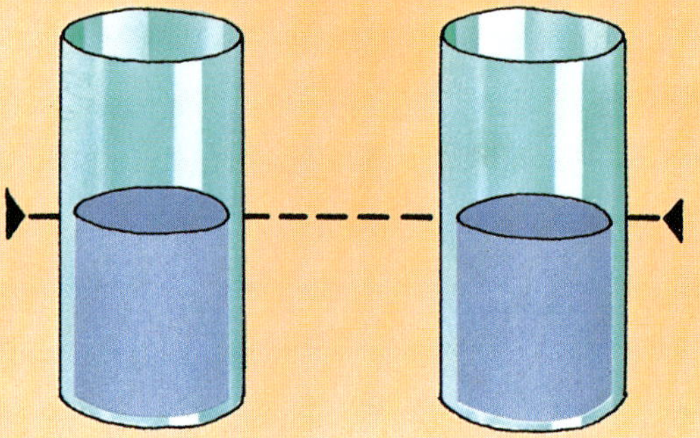

Take the other glass and pour half of the water into a 3rd glass. Repeat this once more.

Now empty the 4th glass so that you have four different amounts of water: ½ full, ¼ full, ⅛ full and one empty.

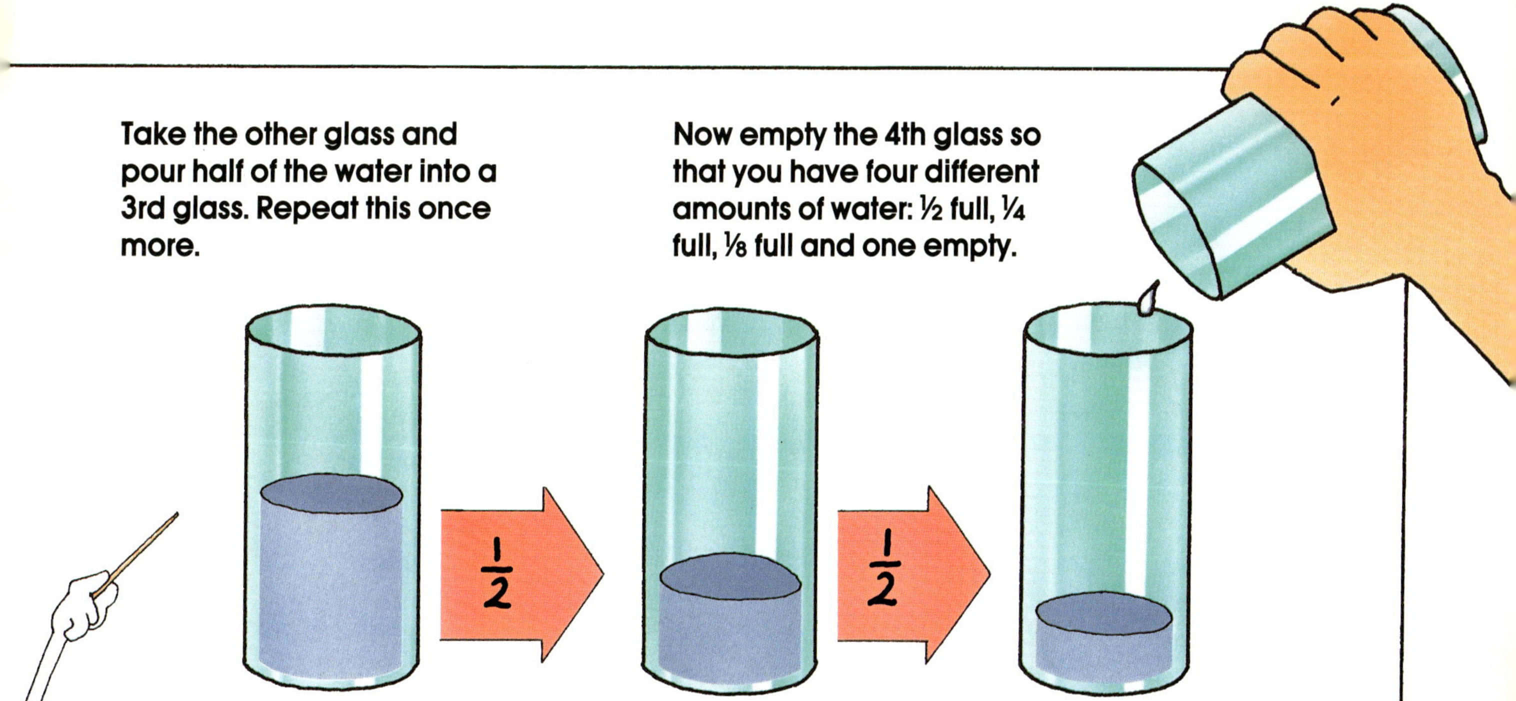

How to play

Now you are ready to play your music. Gently tap the side of each glass with a spoon. Call your glasses A, B, C and D, and write down in which order you have to tap them to make a good tune. Try with more glasses.

JUICE AVERAGES

"Average" is a word which has a special meaning in maths. This activity will help you to understand this meaning. Try it with three friends to make it more fun.

What you need

What to do
Make a mark halfway up four glasses, and fill them up to the mark. Use a ruler to help.

If you have any juice left over, pour it back into its container to empty the jug.

Ask each friend to drink some of the juice – but not all. Now pour all of the remaining juice back into the jug.

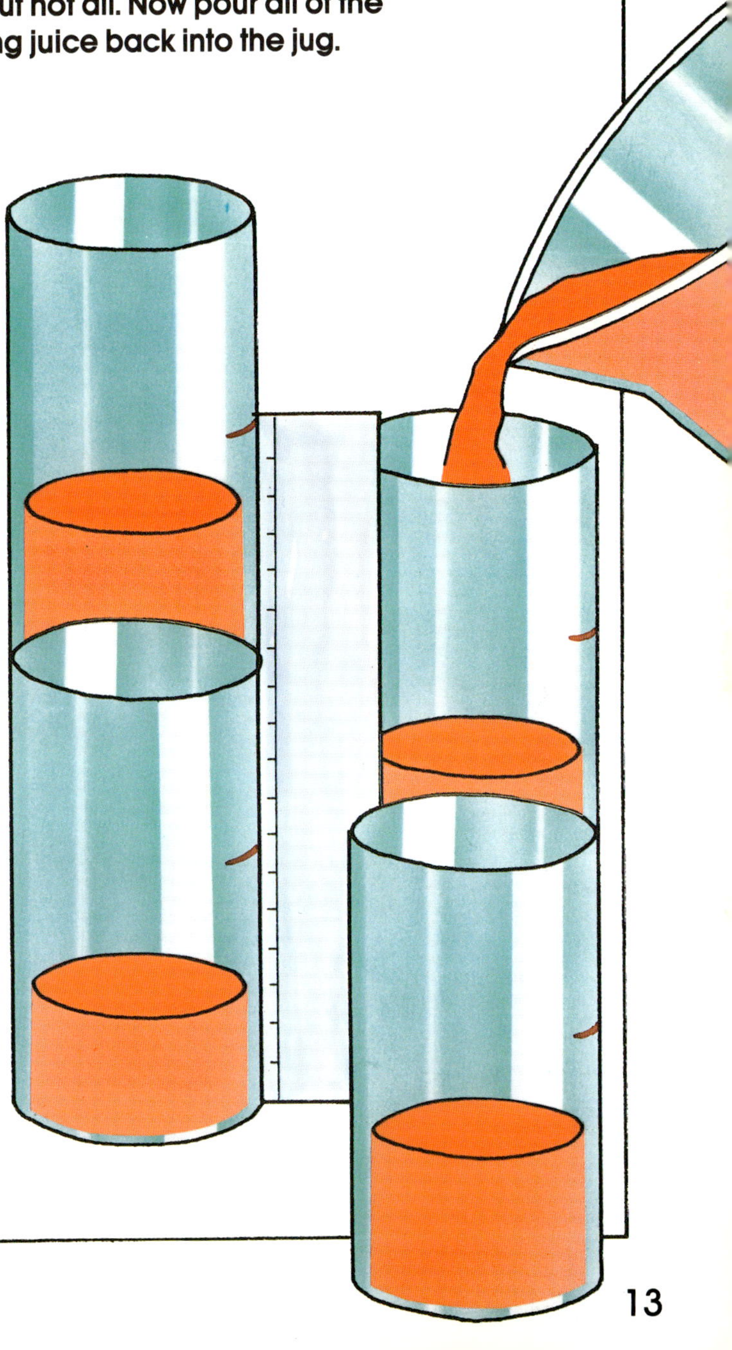

Refill the glasses with equal amounts in each. Use a ruler to measure the distance from the mark on the glass to the juice level. This is the "average" amount your friends drank.

FIREFIGHTER'S LADDER

In this activity we try to work out how many sheets and ladder rungs we need to save people from different floors of a burning building.

What to do
Draw a building like the one below. Make each floor 2cm high. Now draw a ladder with the rungs 1cm apart, and make several 4cm-long sheets and cut them all out.

Sheets and ladders
Four rungs reach two floors. A sheet reaches two floors. How many sheets and rungs are needed for each floor?

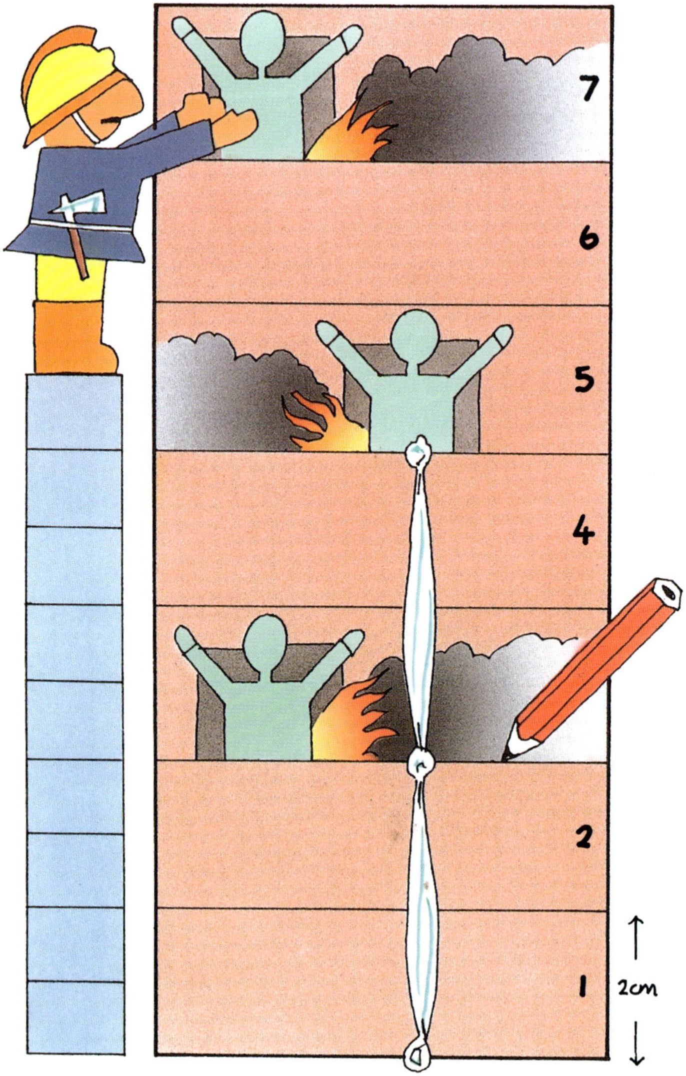

Cut up more floors and ladder rungs so that you can make up some problems of your own to solve.

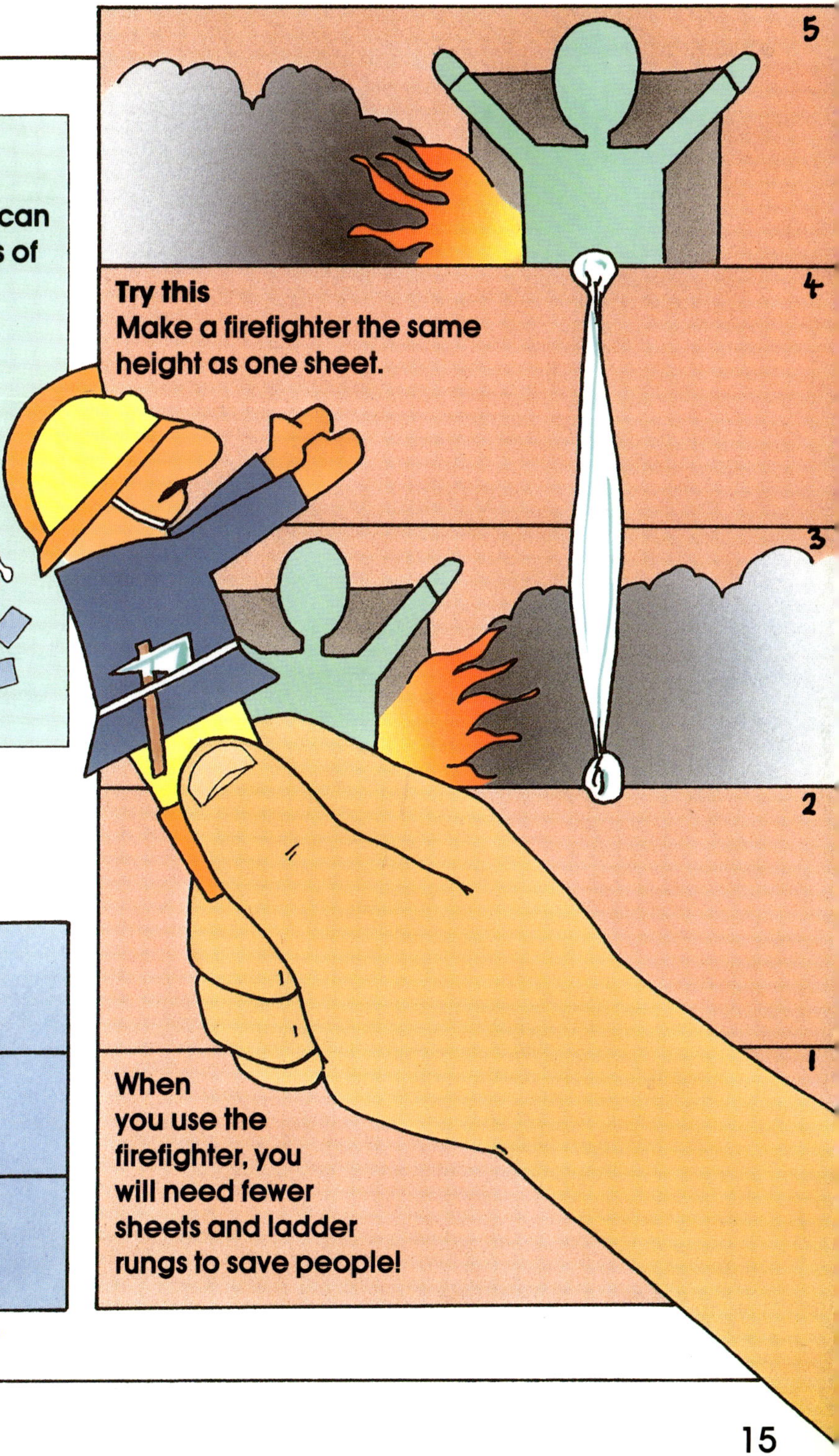

Try this
Make a firefighter the same height as one sheet.

When you use the firefighter, you will need fewer sheets and ladder rungs to save people!

PICTURE JIGSAW

Jigsaw puzzles can keep people busy for hours. They come in all sorts of shapes and sizes. This activity will show you how to make your own jigsaws which you can give to your friends to solve.

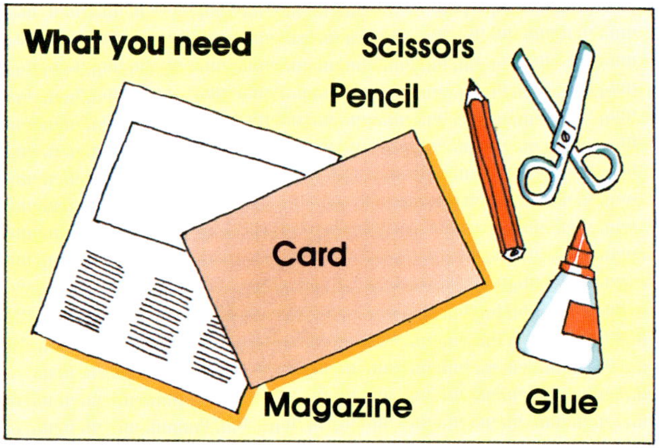

Choose a picture
First choose a picture from a magazine. Cut it out and stick it on to thin card.

Making your jigsaw
Decide how you are going to break up the puzzle. Draw in the outlines for each piece. Cut the pieces out and make sure the edges are smooth. Now you can get a friend to put it together.

How to play
Mix up all the jigsaw pieces. Lay them out on a flat surface so that they all face upwards. Now put the picture back together!

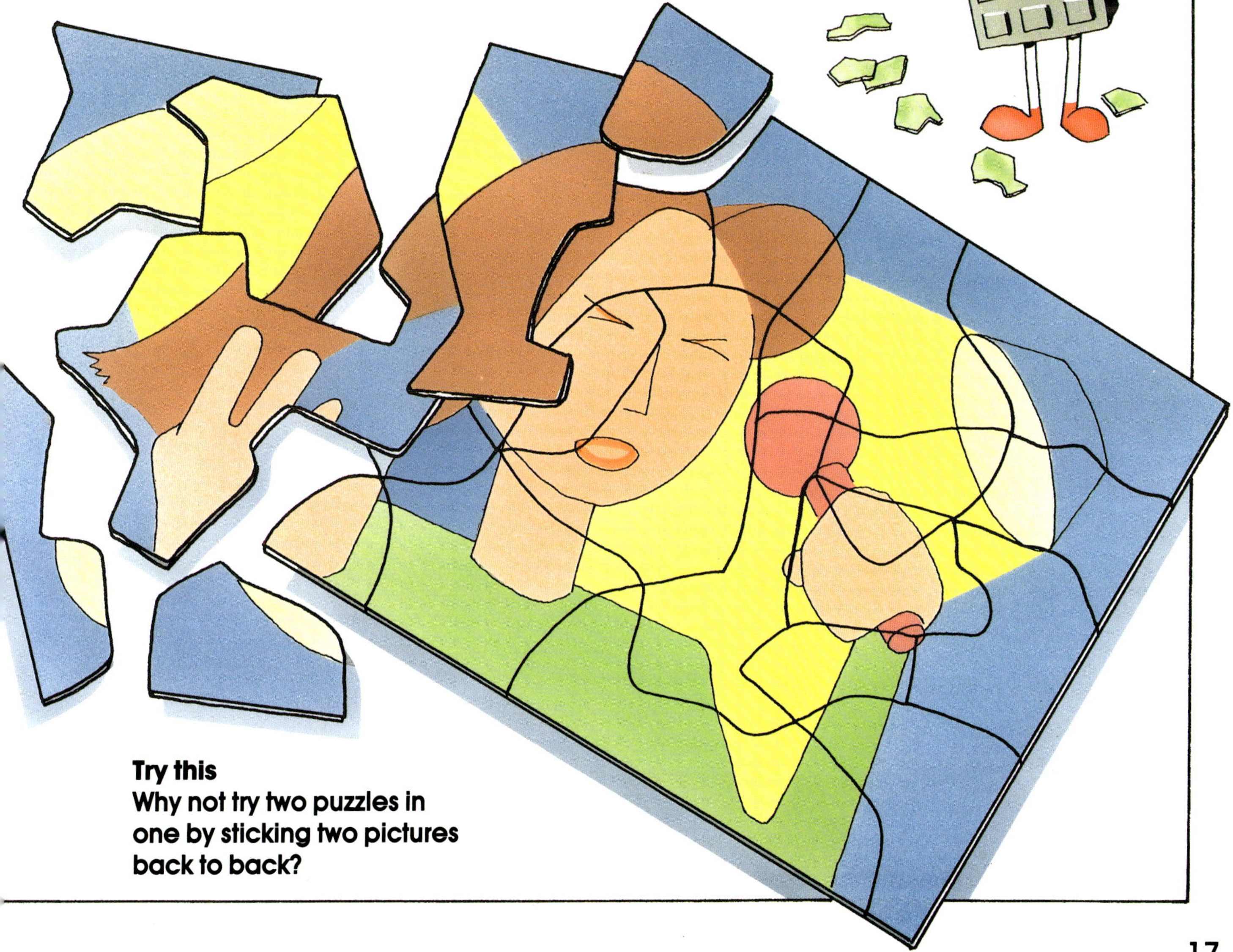

Try this
Why not try two puzzles in one by sticking two pictures back to back?

HIDDEN SQUARES

In this activity, we will be starting with one square and turning it into two or four squares! Remember that all the sides and angles in a square must be equal.

Use your pens to colour in the triangles in two colours, as shown in the picture. Now cut out the eight triangles.

Making it

Copy this picture. Use a ruler to help you draw it exactly right. Go over the lines clearly with your pencil.

Try these
How do you make other squares? Can you make a green square with four green pieces? Try a brown square or four mixed squares.

GUESS THE AGES

This is a brainteaser in which you have to guess people's ages from clues that are given. Good luck!

Everyone does these differently, but it might help to know who is the youngest. Remember that if you add up their ages, they come to 23. If you can't figure it out, there's a hint on the bottom of page 21.

MEENA + GEENA + SHEENA

= **23 YEARS**

HOW OLD IS EACH SISTER?

Geena

WHEN GEENA IS **18**
HOW OLD WILL EACH
OF HER SISTERS BE?

Sheena

WHEN SHEENA IS **20**
HOW OLD WILL EACH
OF HER SISTERS BE?

Meena

WHEN MEENA IS **16**
HOW OLD WILL EACH
OF HER SISTERS BE?

Hint Geena is the same age as the number of letters in her name.

CALENDAR DATES

Have you noticed the way calendars always start on different days? Each month looks similar, but the numbers are in different places. This activity may help you find out why this happens.

What to do
Copy this grid on to paper. Leave out the numbers. Try putting in your own numbers so that the 18th falls on a Monday.

Circle calendar
Try making this circular calendar. Draw the circles with a compass, then copy the other lines from the picture. The arrows show which way to read. Put in the days and then you are ready for the numbers.

Draw your circles with a compass

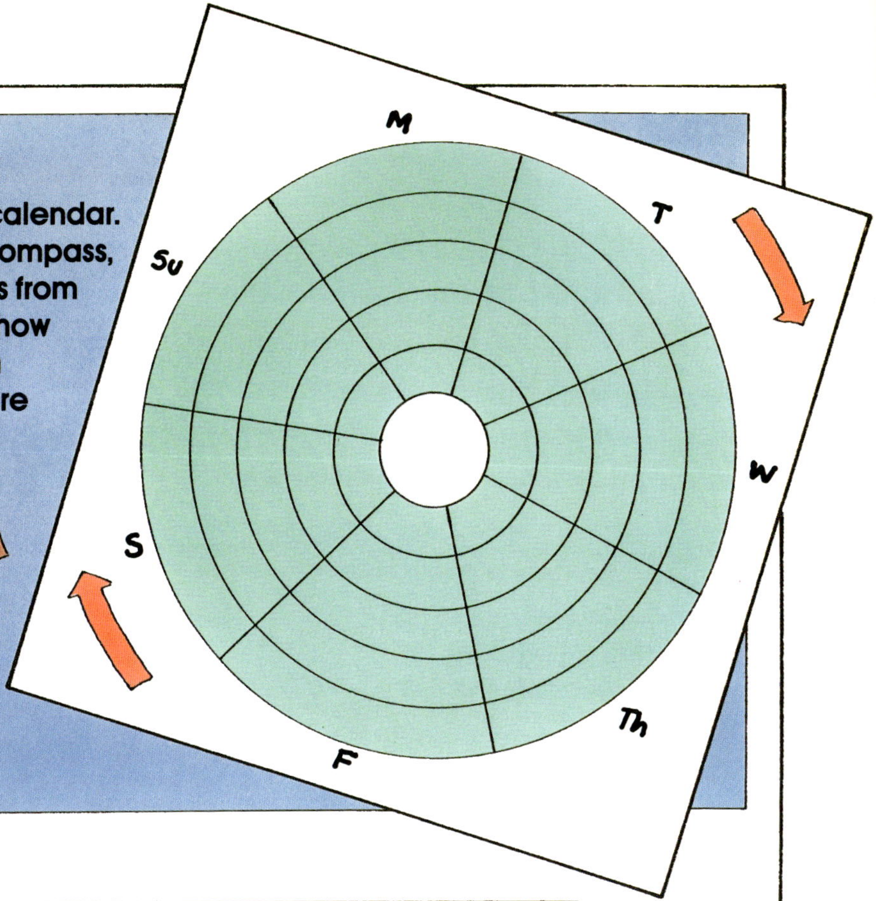

MAKE A CALENDAR WITH

13/11 ON A SUNDAY. WHAT DAY WILL **25/11** BE?

NOW MAKE ONE WITH

7/3 ON A MONDAY. WHAT DAY WILL **1/3** BE?

PERCENTAGES

Percentages are a bit like fractions. Percentage means "part of one hundred", so 20 per cent means 20 parts of one hundred parts. The % sign is often used as a short way of writing per cent. This activity will start you working with percentages.

What you need

Draw a grid like this using a ruler. There should be ten squares on each line.

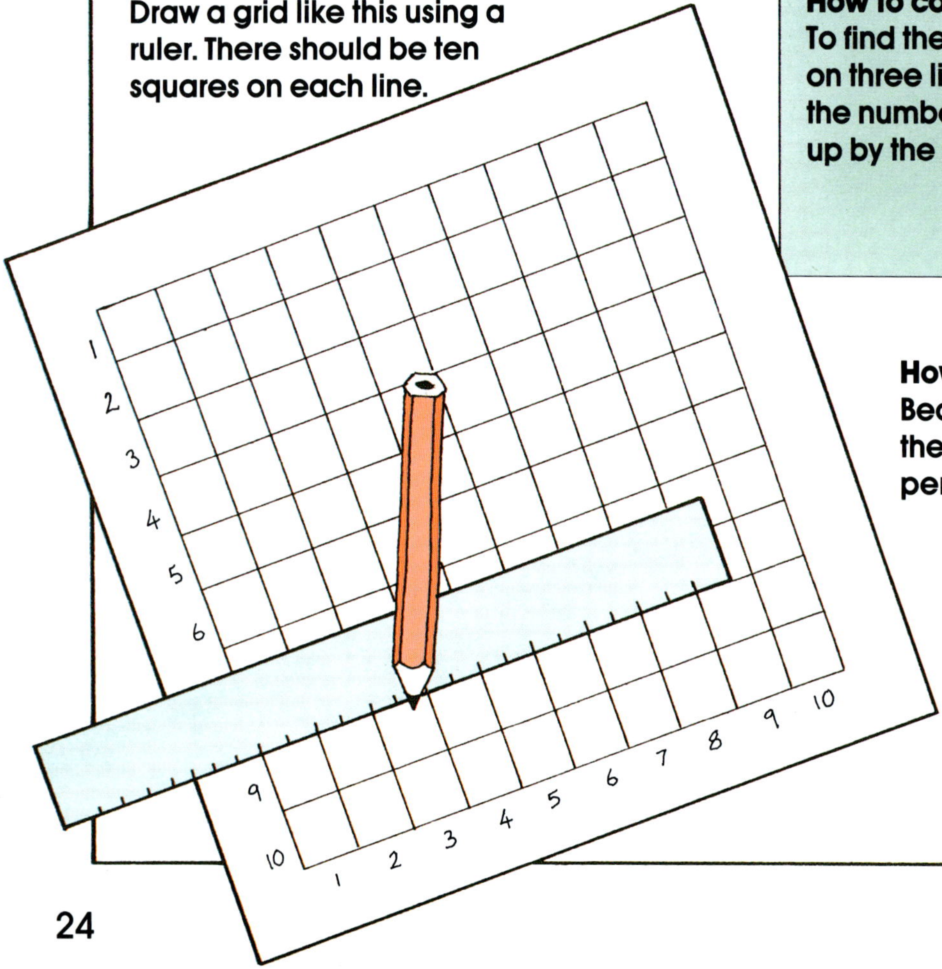

How to count the squares
To find the total squares on three lines, multiply the number of squares up by the number along.

How to count percentages
Because there are 100 squares, the answers are called percentages.

Try this
Using two or more colours, colour in the grid. Cut up your grid into single squares and collect together the different colours.

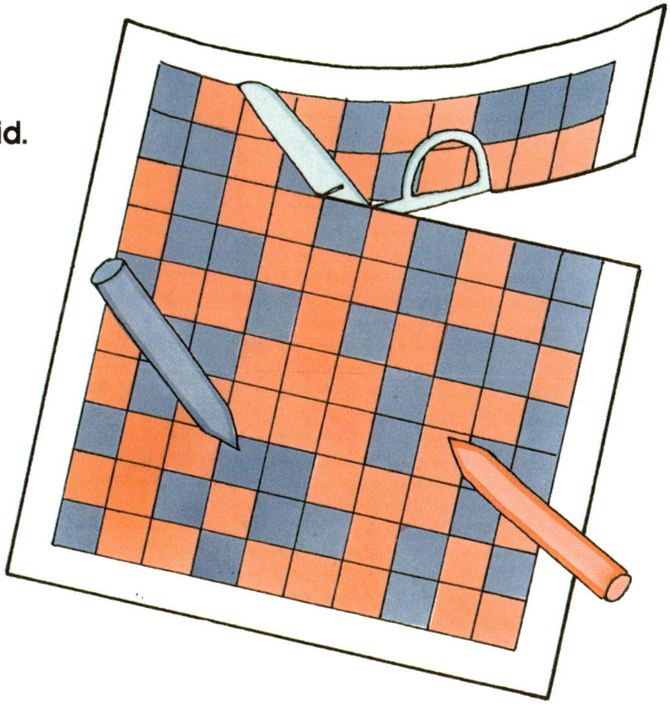

RED

BLUE

How to count
Put each colour into lines of ten (see the diagram). How many full lines do you have? How many squares extra? What percentage of the big square does each colour group represent?

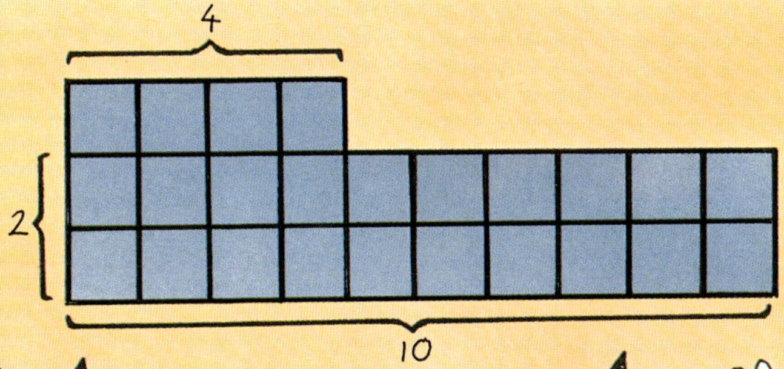

FRACTION PEOPLE

Fraction people is a game for two or three players. You make the cards and then play the game. Look through comics and magazines to find people that you want to draw.

What to do
Copy this outline body on to card and add on clothes, face etc to make your person. Do four pictures like this.

Colour in your pictures and divide two into halves, and two into quarters. Use the size markers (shown left) to help you do this.

Cut along the lines you have drawn and mix the pieces up. Share out the halves and quarters amongst the players.

How to play

Take turns to put down a piece so that you can watch the fraction people growing. You should end up with four funny characters!

Try these

Try some more pictures (maybe fraction animals). This time why not try some different fractions. The size markers will help you.

TOOTHPICK PUZZLE

Toothpick puzzles are easy to make and fun to solve. You can use toothpicks or sticks, or even just draw them as lines on paper. The puzzles can vary – some can represent sums (see below), while others can make patterns (see opposite page).

What you need

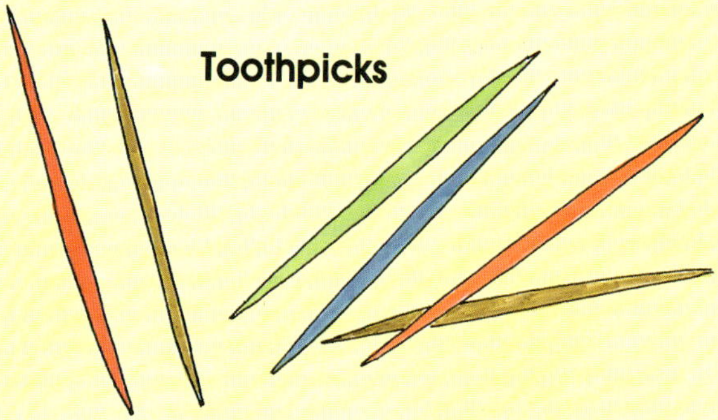

What to do

The puzzle below shows an incorrect sum: 3+1 = 1. By moving only one toothpick, how can you make a sum that works? Remember, any one of the sticks can be moved – those forming the mathematical symbols, as well as those representing the numbers. Try making up other sums for your friends to put right in one move; for example, 1111 + 1 = 111 could become 111 + 1 = 1111 (1 = 1 toothpick).

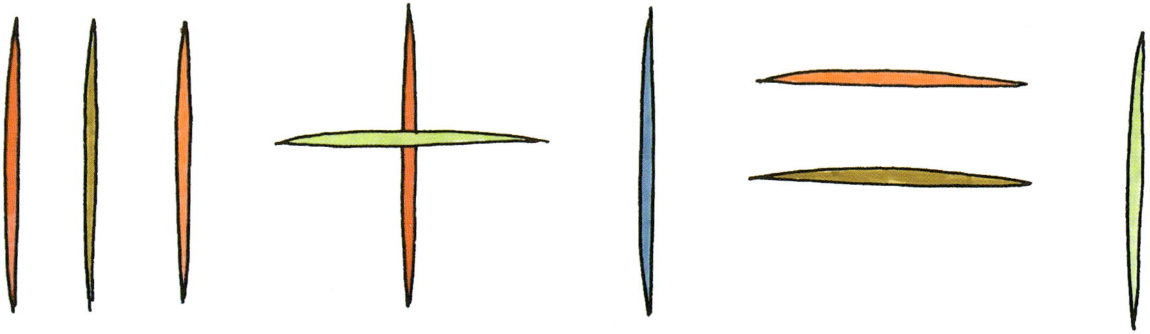

Coal trick
Here the toothpicks represent a shovel, and a pebble is the piece of coal. Can you get the coal out of the shovel without touching the coal and while still keeping a shovel? It can be done by moving only two sticks.

If you can't work these out, turn to pg. 32.

Try this
The puzzle here shows four squares. By moving three of the toothpicks to a new position you can change the pattern to three squares. Can you do it?

GLOSSARY/SYMBOLS

Fractions are what we call pieces from a whole thing (like a cake). One bit out of four is $\frac{1}{4}$, or one quarter. 1/10 means one piece out of ten.

Percentages are like fractions, except they are always out of a hundred pieces. (See the activity on percentage squares, pages 24-25).

Equations are sums that tell us the answers, but that have missing numbers represented by letters. We need to find the missing numbers.

$$8 + x = 10$$
$$x = 10 - 8$$
$$x = 2$$

SOME DIFFERENT WAYS OF WRITING FRACTIONS

FRACTIONS	PERCENTAGES	DECIMALS
1	100%	1
½	50%	0.5
⅓	33.3%	0.33
¼	25%	0.25
⅕	20%	0.2
⅛	12.5%	0.125
1/10	10%	0.1
1/15	6.6%	0.066
1/20	5%	0.05
1/25	4%	0.04

INDEX

ANSWERS

Page 6-7: For 8 people (double the ingredients), for 12 (3 times), for 16 (4 times), for 20 (5 times). Divide the original number of people into the new number of people to find out how many times to multiply the ingredients.

Page 9 For an 8-piece cake, ½ cake = 4 pieces, ¼ cake = 2 pieces, 2 cakes = 16 pieces.

Page 14: ½ sheet or 2 ladder rungs reach one floor.

Page 20: Geena is 5, Sheena is 8 and Meena is 10 yrs. old.

Page 21: (1) Sheena will be 21 and Meena 23.
(2) Geena will be 17 and Meena 22.
(3) Geena will be 11 and Sheena 14.

Page 23: 25/11 will be a Friday. 1/3 will be a Tuesday.

Page 28

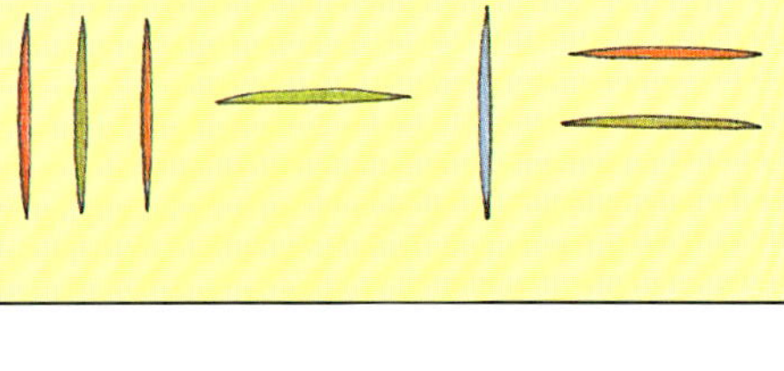

Page 29

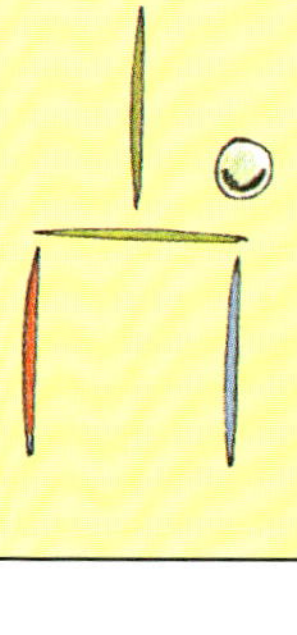